"I have known Eddie Ensley since he was a very young man, and he has always had passion and skill for healing real people with their real sufferings... you are being taught by a master who has practiced this healing work for most of his life, along with his faithful coworker, Deacon Robert Herrmann."

RICHARD ROHR, OFM, *Author of The Universal Christ*

"There is no place in the universe that is as safe and secure as being under the covering of our Creator and Heavenly Father. In this book, *Holding God's Hand: Meditations to Relieve Stress, Worry, and Fear,* Dr. Ensley provides us with a map so we can enter this safe place with ease and be able to escape the emotions that rob us of our happiness, peace, and joy. Dr. Ensley has an intimate relationship with God and his words serve as a life preserver that will rescue you and pull you into the safety of God's arms. He helps you learn how to hold God's hand and how to be set free from worry, stress, and fear. You will love this book!"

RICHARD G. ARNO, PHD,
Founder, National Christian Counselors Assn.

"Deacon Ensley provides uplifting and comforting reflections to strengthen the faith of many in a world full of fear and anxiety. Heartfelt and prayerful, these meditations will help you start the day with the confidence that God is at your side. I am grateful to Deacon Ensley for his continued ministry, and I pray that it will continue to bear great fruit."

BISHOP STEPHEN D. PARKES, *Diocese of Savannah*

"A timely book, with a timeless message, just in time. Eddie points us to rest in God, rather than become consumed by the stress surrounding us. Keep this book close."

DR. ROGER PARROTT, *President, Belhaven University*

"We live in a time of tumult. People need to know that there is hope for them. Deacon Ensley gives clarity on how to turn to the Lord and/or another person to deal with 'chaos' and begin a healing process. He includes some very important tools on how to do this. The book is not theoretical, but Deacon Eddie meets people right where they are in the heart."

DANIEL ALMETER, *Licensed Professional Counselor, Director of Alleluia School of Spiritual Direction*

Deacon Eddie Ensley, PhD
and **Deacon Robert Herrmann**

Holding God's Hand

Meditations

TO RELIEVE STRESS, WORRY AND FEAR

TWENTY-THIRD PUBLICATIONS

twentythirdpublications.com

TWENTY-THIRD PUBLICATIONS
977 Hartford Turnpike Unit A
Waterford, CT 06385
(860) 437-3012 or (800) 321-0411
www.twentythirdpublications.com

Scripture texts, prefaces, introductions, footnotes and cross references
used in this work are taken from the New American Bible, revised edition
© 2010, 1991, 1986, 1970 Confraternity of Christian Doctrine, Inc.,
Washington, DC. All rights reserved.

Cover photo: © stock.adobe.com/Lemonsoup14

ISBN: 978-1-62785-743-7
Printed in the U.S.A.

 A division of Bayard, Inc.

*I dedicate this book
to my Alma Mater, Belhaven University
and my Scripture Professors,*

DR. WALTER ELWELL,

DR. JULIUS SCOTT,

and JOHN AKERS

*I include, especially, some of my
spiritual friends from the University:*

REV. PAUL EVANS,

DR. FRANK COVINGTON,

DR. DANNY MASSIE,

DR. DWYN MOUNGER,

and REV. MORSE UPDEGRAFF

CONTENTS

FOREWORD

Dear Friends,

In John 14:1, our Lord assures...*Do not let your hearts be troubled. You have faith in God; have faith also in me.* As we live in times of great turmoil and uncertainty, these words of Jesus continue to ring true. An encounter with Jesus Christ leads to the ease of the fear and anxiety that plague the world today. Every soul has the ability to find comfort through an encounter with the Risen Lord who invites us to cast our troubles aside and to have faith in God the Father.

Saint Paul invites us to "rejoice in the Lord always" in his letter to the Philippians. True joy is only achieved by our surrendering to the love of God and placing our trust in him. God desires to turn our mourning into joy and wants us to never forget his ability to accomplish it.

For many years, Deacon Ensley has led Parish Missions throughout the country, and through this ministry, has assisted many of the faithful to deepen their faith in Jesus. My hope is that this book of uplifting and comforting reflections will strengthen the faith of many. Heartfelt and prayerful, these meditations will help the reader start the day with confidence that God is at his or her side. I am grateful to Deacon Ensley for his continued ministry, and I pray that it will continue to bear great fruit.

May we meet each day in our prayers and *rejoice in the Lord always!*

MOST REVEREND STEPHEN D. PARKES
Bishop of Savannah

INTRODUCTION

If you picked up this book, likely either you or someone you love is passing through rough times. Perhaps the problem is the constant stress and worry that are easy to feel in this chaotic world of ours. Maybe it is past hurts that left you broken and nag at you even today. It could be the weight of losing someone you loved or a dream you had dearly hoped for. Sadly, for a great many of us, it is all these things.

When we are worried and anxious, stressed, full of fear and uncertainty, certain things have a way of calming and reassuring us. The hand of a friend clasped in ours can ease us. A warm, comforting voice can settle us down. Some Scripture passages have a special ability to deeply still and soften us when the world seems altogether too much for us. Meditations, especially meditations rooted in Scripture and deep prayer, can be like the tender speech of God reaching out to us in our time of need.

When emotions overwhelm us, and life is painfully difficult, God stands ready to infuse us with his calm. So many of us struggle to find peace but don't know where to turn. When emotions overwhelm us, and life is painfully difficult, God yearns for us to entrust our troubles to his care. But so many of us struggle even to translate woes into words.

Each meditation in this book is meant to wrap you in the love of God, to help you truly feel God's presence in your time of need, to help you experience the only place that brings real peace: the welcome of God's outstretched arms.

The meditations can be read daily as devotions. However, they need not be read in order. Instead, you are invited to turn to the topics that speak most to your struggle. In these pages, you will find meditations to help you when you are suffering from stress, worry, fear, healing past trauma, and loneliness.

Each meditation contains a prayer, a Scripture passage, and a short guided prayer journey. You are invited to awaken to the wonder of God within and to set foot on the road to a happier, more peaceful life and a deeper relationship with God.

1

The Love of God Calms Our Souls

"With age-old love I have loved you;
so I have kept my mercy toward you."

JEREMIAH 31:3

The love of God eases our stress and worry, calms us, and stills our souls. God loves us so much that there is no anxiety that cannot be relieved, no mourner who cannot be comforted. His love is the balm that can turn the very shadow of death into morning. May we dare believe this, though our faces be streaked by tears and our chests squeezed with stress.

By frequent meditation on God's forever embrace, we plunge ourselves more and more into his love, the greatest possible grace. How wonderful it is to contemplate the love of a God who forgets as he forgives and drops our selfish actions, when we confess them, into the bottomless depths of the ocean of his love. There they will never be found, remembered, or mentioned into eternity.

It is a spectacular love that nothing can ever halt, nothing can exhaust, nothing can interrupt! It will not let us go. It leaps the gulf of space and bridges time. We cannot earn it or climb a ladder to it. It is not our love that grasps God, but

God's love that grasps us. All he asks is our yes. Nothing can separate us from the love of God.

Prayer

Dear God, unwavering as the affection of a friend, genuine as the love of a mother, your love for me is unalterable. Bathe me in the warm and blessed glow of that love. Help me to trust in it and yield to it. Daily give me glimpses of your loving heart. May I take deep draughts of that love through prayer, sacrament, and Scripture. May I sink down like a child on the pillow of your care.

Guided Meditation

Allow yourself to sit in stillness for a while. The love of God grows thick in your room, easing your muscles, relaxing your soul. Jesus comes and stands beside you, grasping your shoulder firmly with his hand. He tells you he wants to take you on a journey. In your imagination, he takes you back to the creation of the cosmos and Adam and Eve. He tells you without words that he is ever making you new, and because of the new and fresh love he gives, your life can be bright with happiness. He takes you to the scene where he brought Lazarus back to life. He lets you know he can restore you, too, when the anxiousness of fear, stress, and worry hold sway in your life. He takes you to his crucifixion and lets you know that is the depth of love he has for you. He carries you to his resurrection, where the brilliance of eternity will reign forever, and you, too, can enter into glory.

2

Hold on to God's Hand

*They that hope in the Lord will renew
their strength, they will soar on eagles' wings;
They will run and not grow weary;
walk and not grow faint.* ISAIAH 40:31

There is something grounding and calming in holding hands with another person. Holding someone's hand can express love and boost fortitude. A mother may take the hand of a child who is receiving an injection from a doctor to lessen the child's fear of the needle. Hands held by couples can be an electric sign of devotion and commitment. Someone holding your hand when you are distraught can soothe you and let you know that everything will be okay. A chaplain holding the hand of the bed-bound and sick can lift their spirits and let them know that God cares.

What would it be like for you to hold God's hand? I imagine it would be an invigorating stream of calm and love spreading from your hand to every particle of your body and the whole of your soul. It would quiet your distress and warm your soul. When you are stressed and the storms of worry have taken over, that handclasp with God can finally quiet down your spirit.

Any time anxiety troubles you or fear bends you over with worry, you can reach out and fasten your hand to God's hand. When your vitality fades and helplessness takes you over, grip the hand of the one who can always help.

When Jesus walked the earth, the touch of his hand comforted and healed. Only in heaven will we know how many hands he held. Jesus said, "I came so that they might have life and have it more abundantly" (John 10:10). His hand conveys that life.

Prayer

Dear Lord, I hand over to you my tension, my fears, my stress. Soften my heart with your nearness. Shine your light along the roads I take. And always, in every place, may I soothe, comfort, and cherish others in the way that you soothe, comfort, and cherish me. As I face my anxieties, help me become an emblem of your healing, a quiet presence along the way, one who comforts others with your love.

Guided Meditation

Sit relaxed in your chair. Notice your inhaling and exhaling breath. The very act of breathing reminds you of the breath of the Spirit. When you breathe in, imagine the peacefulness of God entering with your breath, deeply relaxing you. When you breathe out, visualize negativity, fatigue, anxiety, worry, and tension being breathed out. The muscles of your face grow loose and relaxed, deeply relaxed. God's love unties the tight muscles of your chest and torso. Your arms and legs grow limp with God's ease. Sit there calmly. Jesus comes and stands beside you. He clasps your hand, and you feel the vigor of his love as he rejuvenates you.

3

Worry Less and Pray More

Have no anxiety at all, but in everything, by prayer and petition...make your requests known to God. **PHILIPPIANS 4:6**

We humans worry. We worry about everything...home, family, health, war, the pandemic, our job, and finances. We fret about the future.

When we worry, it causes us harm. It damages our physical and mental health, lessens our productivity, affects our love and care for others, and makes it hard for us to think efficiently. Worry immobilizes us. As a result, we do nothing or even do something foolish.

You may ask, does this mean I shouldn't be concerned about things? Yes, of course you should. But there is a vast difference between worry and concern. Authentic concern moves you to constructive action.

When we concentrate on our problems, we worry, but when we concentrate on God and his love, we replace the worry with peace. We need to look at where our focus is. Focusing on the details of the bad makes it hard to see the vast good.

Don't worry about anything; instead, pray about everything. Then you will experience God's peace. Tell your needs to God, perhaps even list them.

When you are in the middle of the storms and thunder of worry, turn your heart and mind toward Jesus by telling him what is going on. Let him fill you with his warmth. He can whisper in your heart, "You are my beloved. I treasure you. I am larger than your worry. I have a plan for you. I am leading you. I am directing you. Don't be afraid of the future; I am already there. I hold you in the palm of my hand."

Prayer

Dear Lord, it is so easy to worry, yet no amount of my worrying is going to change things. The bottom line is that you, Lord, are in charge. Teach me to worry less and pray more. When worries come, Lord, guide me in turning them over to you, one by one. Help me to center my heart on your goodness and wonder. Guide me to Scriptures that lead me into your loving care.

Guided Meditation

As you are seated, the peace of God gathers all around you and flows within you. Rest...relax awhile. Now you notice a big gunny sack filled with heavy stones sitting beside you. You have to carry that sack around wherever you go. The stones are your worries. Jesus comes and stands in front of you. You see a look of concern and compassion on his face. You relax even more, growing deeply peaceful. You touch the very hem of his garment and feel his love radiating within you. Jesus looks down at the gunny sack full of stones sitting beside you and says, "Give those to me." Each stone represents a worry. You pick up a heavy stone, name a worry, and place it in his hand. He takes the stone into his heart, where it disappears into that living flame of love.

4

Give Your "What Ifs" to God

"So do not worry and say, 'What are we to eat?'
or 'What are we to drink?' or 'What are we to wear?'...
But seek first the kingdom [of God] and his righteousness,
and all these things will be given you besides. Do not worry
about tomorrow; tomorrow will take care of itself.
Sufficient for a day is its own evil."
MATTHEW 6:31, 33–34

It can seem like disaster is looming on every corner at times. Your boss doesn't smile at you in the parking lot, and you wonder, "What if I lose my job?" You hear of people dying of various illnesses, and you worry, "What if my loved ones get sick?" You hear of wildfires, tornadoes, mass shootings, and you worry about terrible things happening to you or those you care about.

With all this worry, it is hard to savor the joy of sunshine on your face or the happy laughter of your toddler. You are being robbed of the freshness of each moment, and God seems far away.

What if something awful does happen? St. Paul says, "Neither death, nor life...nor present things, nor future things, nor powers...nor any other creature will be able to separate us from the love of God in Christ Jesus our Lord" (Romans 8:38–39). God's arms of calm and comfort are always open to us when "what ifs" take us over. Let us rush into those arms.

Prayer

Dear Lord, my anxiety is no mystery for you, for you have entered fully into all this world's stresses and worries. Even when I am overcome with "what ifs," you are there. Anxiety is no puzzle for you, for you have entered fully into all this world's stress. You hold my tears. You remember my sighs of worry. Even when I think myself afflicted on all sides, you are there. May my story be ever tied to yours.

Guided Meditation

Imagine that you are floating on your back on a limitless ocean, the ocean of God's love. You feel so safe. Calm waves gently lapping over your stomach and legs soothe you. It is so restful to rest in God's peace. You safely float lower into the ocean where there are no waves; all is tranquil and still in the deeps. You feel as if there is no end to the depths of this ocean, just as there is no end to the depths of God's love. As you rest there, tensions, anxieties, all your "what ifs" slip out of you into the ocean. You return to being seated in your chair. Jesus holds your hand, and you sit there awhile, resting in his peace.

5

Jesus Provides Rest for the Weary

I was hard pressed and falling, but the LORD came to my help. The LORD, my strength and might, has become my savior. PSALM 118:13–14

Sometimes a little bit of stress can help motivate us. It keeps me at the keyboard writing my books when I am facing a deadline. Stress encourages me to spend quality time in my prayer chair because I know that my ministry and writing dry up when I don't soak in God's love in prayer. But most of the time, I find stress barreling me toward burnout. I have so many tasks to accomplish and so little time. I feel so inadequate. More often, stress is a weighty burden rather than a motivator.

What an amazing relief it is when I remember that I don't carry my burdens alone. Jesus helps me. He instructs us, "Come to me, all you who labor and are burdened, and I will give you rest" (Matthew 11:28).

God doesn't want us to live in continual stress. He wants us to walk daily in the certainty of his rest. We should allow the stress to push us into his arms, where he removes our tensions and burdens.

What is weighing on you now: problems at work, making sure your children catch up in their education and social connections after setbacks during the pandemic, worry about the latest strain of a virus or widening war, extended families being torn apart by the polarization or the demonizing of others that is a part of our current culture? St. Peter's words offer us a way out: "Cast all your worries upon him because he cares for you" (1 Peter 5:7).

Prayer

Dear Lord, you are the vanquisher of stress. You always stand ready to lift the heavy pack I carry on my back. Lord, I put into your hands all things that are too heavy for me to carry alone. Whenever stress rattles me, remind me of the warmth and peace that come from turning to you.

Guided Meditation

You are seated. Take in a deep breath. As you exhale, breathe out tiredness, stress, worry, fears. You are surrounded by a beautiful light, the light of God's ease and rest. You breathe in the light. It flows through your body, calming you, relaxing you, bringing God's peace to you, filling your body and soul with the brightness of God. After the light has passed through you, Jesus comes and stands beside you. You see his wounds and the light coming out of those wounds. He says to you, "It is through your wounded parts that the light will shine out more brightly on others in the same way my light has shone on you." He asks what burdens and stresses weigh you down. You tell him. Then he invites you, "Pass them over to me." Rest in the peace of God.

6

How God Can Take Our Fears Away

"For I am the LORD, *your God, who grasp your right hand; It is I who say to you, 'Do not fear, I will help you.'"* ISAIAH 41:13

When our fears afflict us, we don't have to sit there squeezed in their icy grip. All too often, we want to run or distract ourselves from the dread that can haunt us. We don't want to look at them directly. Instead of this, we can say, "Lord, I want to deal with this. Help me." He will give us the courage to deal with our fears with his hand in ours.

Listing our fears is one way to do this. Looking directly at them begins to take away their sway over us. When they are in the light, they do not look as large and alarming. We can then take them to the God who promised to bear our burdens. His comforting, healing Spirit can ease us in the same way a parent's embrace can calm a little child amid a wild thunderstorm.

In the gospels, Christ gave 125 commands. In the most common of these, twenty-one urge us not to be afraid or to worry. The second most common command, "love God," is mentioned only eight times.

These commands suggest that with God's help, we have the power of choice: with his help, we can cast our fears aside. We can choose to let those fears keep rumbling through us, or we can say "stop" and put them into the comforting arms of the One who loves us without measure.

Prayer

Dear Lord, like us, you experienced fear. In Gethsemane, you got your terror out in the open, into the light, to the Father, who heard you and took you through it all to resurrection. Help me to look directly at my fears and the reasons why I fear. It is so easy to let fear take hold. Help me to trust in your mercy. Send me to the many comforting Scripture passages whose very words can calm my soul. Lead me to talk over my fears with trusted others so I will not be alone in my fears.

Guided Meditation

It is a beautiful day. You stand in a grassy field that is so beautiful, it reminds you of the pastures of the Twenty-third Psalm. You feel God's huge presence all around you, absorbing tension and anxiety. The muscles of your body ease and relax; your worries dissolve. You hear the sound of someone walking toward you. You turn, and there is Jesus. He embraces you and you feel the enormity of his love. He tells you, "I want to show you the glory of heaven." You two begin to float upward. You are surrounded by holy, heavenly light. You hear the singing of angels. You know this is a place of forever beauty and comfort. In the light of heaven, you name your fears one by one, and they disappear in the light of glory.

7

He Will Not Fail You or Forsake You

"Be strong and steadfast...It is the LORD who goes before you; he will be with you and will never fail you or forsake you. So do not fear or be dismayed." **DEUTERONOMY 31:7-8**

A raging storm threatened to sink the boat. Then the disciples saw Jesus walking on the water. Jesus called to Peter, "Come." Peter looked at Jesus and placed one foot in front of the other. He was able to walk on the water. But then his attention turned to the heavy winds and the raging waves. He lost his trust and faith and began to sink. In desperation, he cried out to Jesus, who saved him (Matthew 14:22–33).

It is so easy for us to think negatively. Maybe there are real storms in our lives, such as the one the disciples faced in the boat. But even amid trials and tribulations, we make things so much worse with our negative thinking. Our fretting minds can easily see a cyclone when it is just a passing thundershower.

While we can and will be buffeted by storms, we must never forget that Jesus comes walking on the water toward us even when we face the worst news. As long as our attention is fixed on God and his goodness, we can experience his enduring comfort. He helps us walk on the water of our difficulties. In those times when we take our eyes off him and sink, Jesus can reach out his hand and pick us up. He is there to comfort us and keep us stable with the tenderness of his power. He can calm us in the middle of the lightning and waves.

How do we keep our attention on God? By thinking of him often, singing hymns, praying daily, reading spiritual works, and caring for the marginalized and lonely. With our eyes firmly on Jesus, we can weather any storm.

Prayer

Dear Lord, too often I keep my eyes on the storm rather than on the calm you provide. Remind me daily that you can take my hand. With you, I can walk steadily even when the ground is moving under me. You walked on the water; you raised Lazarus from the dead; you fed the five thousand. You can calm the whirlwinds in my life.

Guided Meditation

Sit quietly in a chair. With each inhalation, you breathe in tranquility. When you exhale, you breathe out negativity. The abiding calm of God settles around you. Your muscles let go of tightness and grow limp in God's nearness. Your heart beats calmly and evenly. Your breath grows deep and regular. Jesus comes up beside you and takes your hand, and you absorb the stillness of his peace. You tell him about some of the storms in your life; the weight of your worry lessens. With his hand in yours, you feel as if you could walk on water.

8

Finding Your Happy Place Inside

"Peace I leave with you; my peace I give to you.
Not as the world gives do I give it to you.
Do not let your hearts be troubled or afraid."
JOHN 14:27

Stress can ruin our happiness, break up our families, and cause us to push God away. God does not will stress for us. Jesus wishes to hold our hand when we are bathed in stress. He said, "My peace I leave with you," not "my stress I leave with you."

Stress is not a hobgoblin outside us that causes us to be afraid and full of anxiety. Rather, psychologists tell us that stress is our response to life and originates within us. They suggest rewiring our thoughts to drive out stress. As a way of doing that, they often speak of "going to a happy place inside" when stress raises its fearsome presence. They speak of this as an almost magical place within that we can run to when things seem too much for us.

People interpret this "happy place" inside in different ways, but I am sure that like me, many people see this as a place inside where God shares his safety and heart-mending presence. A place where we can commune on the deepest level of consciousness with the One who loves us with such tender care that he shares his unspeakable gladness along with his love. This is the place we should rush to inside of us.

I think the psalmist was speaking of just such a place where he shares, "You who dwell in the shelter of the Most High, who abide in the shade of the Almighty, Say to the LORD, 'My refuge and my fortress, my God in whom I trust'" (Psalm 91:1–2).

We have a choice between struggling and fighting with the circumstances that cause us stress or asking God to embrace us as we place our struggles in his care.

Prayer

Dear Lord, there are times when stress can turn my world upside down. I know you do not wish me to be stressed. Instead, you wish to dwell in my heart in peace. If I but let you, you can create a sacred space within me which I can go to for refuge. Your kingdom is within. May I let you reign there. May I choose your presence rather than the stress of fearing and worrying. Your presence within is like a candle lit in my heart. May I daily turn to the light of that candle.

Guided Meditation

Sit comfortably in your chair. Allow the deep relaxation of God's presence within you to ease your torso, your muscles, your limbs. Look straight ahead: you see Jesus standing there. You can see the fiery sacred heart in his chest. That heart beats with an indescribable love. He beckons you, saying, "Draw near." He asks you to place your hand on his heart. As you touch that heart, you touch the love that created the cosmos, the love that died for you and was resurrected. Now you take that same hand and place it on your chest, on your heart spot. You feel a burning in your heart and know that this warmth is your safe place within.

9

Jesus Understands Our Fear

God is our refuge and our strength,
an ever-present help in distress. Thus we
do not fear, though earth be shaken and
mountains quake to the depths of the sea.

PSALM 46:2–3

Sometimes fear is based in a horrible reality, such as finding out your spouse has cancer and has two months to live, or your teenage child will be sentenced to prison for killing a family in a car accident while drunk. Jesus knew fear, the scariest kind of fear, as he encountered a real worst-case scenario. He faced capture, mockery, lashes with a whip full of glass shards, and merciless torture on a cross. This wasn't a fear blown out of proportion; it was as real as his heartbeat or his breath.

Jesus did two things to deal with that anxiety. As *The Message* version of the Bible puts it: "He plunged into a sink-hole of suffocating darkness" (Mark 14:33). First, he faced it. Second, he prayed. In the Garden of Gethsemane, Jesus faced the ultimate fear with a raw and honest prayer: "Abba, Father," he cried out, "everything is possible for you. Please take this cup of suffering away from me. Yet I want your will to be done, not mine" (Mark 14:36).

Torture and death were not the last word for Jesus. Resurrection and consolation came on the third day. And resurrection can come for us. Awareness of God's triumph over all our worst-case scenarios can soothe and calm us even in the sinkhole. As the psalmist tells us, "At dusk weeping comes for the night, but at dawn there is rejoicing" (Psalm 30:6). We can pour out our agony, praying, "Not my will but yours be done." Even in the sinkhole, the tenderness of Jesus' compassion can fill us, because he has faced what we face. He understands our fear.

Prayer

Dear Lord, when I must face hard and awful things in my life, remind me to cry out my fearful agony to you. You will listen and not abandon me. You will walk hand in hand with me in the sinkholes of life. As I expose to you the reasons why I am fearful, you can give me a deeply felt experience of resurrection. You can touch me with your wounded hands, your wounds now emitting everlasting light. Teach me to put all my fears, large and small, in those hands. Lord, you pull us toward an ocean of everlasting light and hope. Even in our most distressing times, the New Jerusalem, where all tears will be washed away, can descend into our hearts. Help us to pass on this hope to others. Amen.

Guided Meditation

In your imagination, go to the Palestine of Jesus' time. Place yourself beside Jesus on a mountain, where he will pray all night. You move close beside him. It is as though the air around him is thick with love and the letting go of fear. You feel safe—so safe that you reach out and touch his robe. Hold tightly to his robe and allow the love-filled stillness of Jesus' prayer to flow through your hand, to your heart, to your whole body. Experience that wordless sense of communion that calms even the most rugged fears.

10

Pour Out Your Hearts

Trust God at all times, my people!
Pour out your hearts to God our refuge!
PSALM 62:9

The phrase "pour out your hearts," found in Psalm 62:9, has always resonated deeply within me. Pouring out our hearts to others or to God can empty us, leaving us feeling deeply loved, understood, and calmed beyond expectation. There are times when our hearts are so full of distress that it seems as though we are about to break. It may be the sorrow of loss, anxiety, disappointment, guilt, anger—any number of pressures that can build up within us until we are bathing in worry.

When such stress overcomes us, we have the ability to choose: we can either keep it inside and plug away with it as best we can, or we can turn to God or another person. June, a friend of mine, poured her heart out to me recently about how grief-stricken she's been since her father died. She could have just mentioned it in passing, but instead she freely shared the pain in her heart—a much healthier choice. Pouring out your entrenched stress or anguish to a trusted friend, clergy member, or counselor can lead to a great emptying of stress.

In prayer, pouring out your heart means speaking freely about your private and most deeply felt emotions to God. It means washing your earthly worries away, day after day, and confiding your most deeply held sorrows to him. If you struggle to find the words, you may wish to free-write your emotions as they come, putting them in the form of a written prayer. However you pray, God always listens with unfathomable compassion. You can trust God in any place and at any time when it is rough going for you. In him, you will find relief and rest.

Prayer

Dear Jesus, you poured out the agony of your emotions to the Father. Help me to likewise pour out my distresses large and small. Grant me the courage to shout, to cry in your presence, to let out all the raw emotions, for you are a refuge, a safe haven, when the storms rumble and threaten.

Guided Meditation

Sit comfortably. Sense the deep tranquility that is God's peace. You can pour out your heart to him, telling him of your stresses large and small. The words of confusion and pain now tumble out of you as you entrust him with your hidden secrets. His balm comforts your soul. You empty out. His goodness fills you. Your emotions grow still. The air you breathe reminds you of the Spirit. You feel light, so very light—light enough to float. You find yourself lifting upward, free of anything holding you down. You are held high by the very presence of God. You know now that you can come to him anytime and pour out your heart to him.

11

God Is Near the Brokenhearted

The LORD is close to the brokenhearted,
saves those whose spirit is crushed.
PSALM 34:19

Maybe you feel that the word "broken" can, at times, be used to describe you. Imagine a pane of transparent glass that has been shattered. It is as though the large clear glass window is the eye of our soul. This is the window through which we see God, others, and our entire world. This window is easily broken. A pebble of hurt, perhaps a parent's verbal abuse, hitting up against it caused it to shatter.

Other pebbles can strike, such as being bullied or the pain of the breakup of your first romance in high school. Sometimes a big rock, a divorce or major loss, causes a hole that streaks out over the entire window. It can become nearly impossible to see clearly through the window. Only God has the power to repair the cracks and provide the healing we need.

I think of Jake, whose marriage was falling apart and who suffered flashbacks from combat. Deacon Robert led him in a meditation in which Christ sat beside him, his light surrounding Jake, absorbing his pain. Afterward, Jake told me he felt better about himself than he had in years. He said, "I have never felt such peace. Jesus was more real than the couch I sat on, and I felt his firm hand rest on my shoulder. I feel he can knit me back together again despite my brokenness." He went on to develop a healing prayer life, started seeing a therapist, and made decisions that put him on track for a happy and fulfilled life.

Scripture promises that God will build the brokenhearted back stronger than before. The prophet Isaiah says God will give those who mourn and are broken "oil of gladness instead of mourning, a glorious mantle instead of a faint spirit" (Isaiah 61:3). When you feel broken, know that God can heal you.

Prayer

Dear Lord, sometimes I feel so broken that it is hard to believe I can be healed. The wounds are too deep. There are too many shattered pieces to be put back together. But you can work miracles. You can take what is broken and make it beautiful. I want to be made well. Please heal my brokenness and make me whole. Amen.

Guided Meditation

Allow the healing love of God to sweep over you, warming you, carrying you into the sacred relaxation that only God can bring. Now, in your imagination, go back to the Palestine of Jesus' time. You are sitting near the pool of Bethesda mentioned in the fifth chapter of the Gospel of John. You are broken by illness and paralysis, sitting on your mat. Around you are similarly broken humans struggling to get in the pool when the waters are stirred and believed to have healing properties. You have wanted to get in that pool for many years but have had no one bring you into the pool. Jesus comes: he tells you to take up your mat and walk. The warmth of healing shoots through your whole body, making whole that which was broken. You get up, take up your mat, and then, with indescribable joy, begin to walk. Return to the present moment. Jesus reminds you that you can tell him daily of your emotional brokenness and he will calm you into healing.

12

God Wants to Soothe Our Souls

*May the God of hope fill you with all joy and
peace in believing, so that you may abound in hope
by the power of the holy Spirit.* ROMANS 15:13

It is in the awareness of God's loving nearness that the heaving ocean within us becomes like a summer's sea. Talking with God daily brings that nearness. Ideally, each day will be one long heartfelt talk with our Creator, but it is important to set aside a special part of the day for prayer. Even the smallest things in our lives we can commend to the one who cares so much that he numbers the very hairs on our heads. God wants to hear us as surely as a grandparent wants to hear a grandchild's voice, as surely as the beloved wants to hear the lover's whisper.

There is no need to fret over what to say. Trust the Spirit to give you the words.

Communicating any unrest we may have to God soothes that unrest. Instead of holding on to your sorrow, speak to him about it. God can relieve half of it, plus the bitterness associated with it, when you simply share it with him.

Take time each day to make acts of contrition and repentance. To confess is to be forgiven. The moment that the consciousness of not being what God wants us to be rises in the heart and we confess, heaven comes to still and soothe our souls.

We should also include others in our prayers, especially the most distressed. It is in taking others' needs to God that we cease to brood over our own troubles. It is in wiping their tears that we forget to weep. God wants us all to be at peace.

Prayer

Dear Lord, you are intimate to us. You are closer to us than our breath or heartbeat. You care about the minutest things in our lives. Help me to open our days to your nearness by talking with you. Remind me of the beauty of this world and inspire me to find you in it and praise you for it. Thank you for all the ways your love has cradled and soothed me in the past. Implant in me a fully felt gratitude for all you do for me, and remind me to tell you about it every day. Forgive me when my prayer centers on myself alone. Widen my prayer to include others, reaching out to them in the prayerful spirit you embed in my heart. Amen.

Guided Meditation

As you sit in your chair, God's nearness moves your heart, eases your muscles, relaxes your body, calms your mind. Jesus comes and sits in front of you. He places his palms on your palms. A profound love passes from his heart to his hands and then into your hands and body. You feel safe, so very safe, being with him. You tell him about your day.

13

How to Let God Heal Past Hurts

"Before I formed you in the womb I knew you,
before you were born I dedicated you."
JEREMIAH 1:5

Joyful memories from our past bring the grace of those times into the present. But, for most of us, some parts of our past are pained. For some of us, a great many of our early memories bring anxiety. We may have grown up with putdowns from our parents rather than guidance and affirmation. Perhaps our early years were lived in a troubled home. We recall times when others shamed and belittled us and times when we looked for nurture and found an icy coldness instead. When we have been verbally abused as children and told we are failures, as adults we can have a player in our head looping the words "You are no good...you are a failure, a loser."

The way we relate today reflects our early home life. Disjointed relationships now often reveal a need for healing the wounds of early relationships. We human beings seem programmed to replay the past in the here and now. As William Faulkner put it, "The past is never dead. It's not even past."

Ultimately, only the medicine of God's love can take away the sting of those painful memories. We can soak up that love in the silence of prayer. We can read the many Scriptures that are especially full of God's love and let that love sink into the marrow of our bones. We can invite Jesus with us into the hurtful memories and let him pour out his curative love there. In short, we can take sunbaths in the love of God and allow that love to rearrange us.

Prayer

You knew and loved me in the womb. You have loved me in your lavish forgiveness. You abide in the center of my soul. Thank you for the good and wonderful parts of my past. I also have my sorrowful mysteries. Your arms around me, assuring me of your tender warmth, can be with me when hurtful memories come up. Free me from the past, so that I may be able to reach out in love to my neighbors, family, friends, and the hurting ones who most need your love. May your mending love help me to see people clearly and not just through the lens of the past. In you, with you, through you, reaching out to others. Amen.

Guided Meditation

As you have read this meditation, painful memories from your past may have emerged. Imagine that you are seated and that Jesus takes your hand. Soft, warm relaxation flows from his body into yours, a love that slowly begins to melt away any feelings of hurt from the past. You feel the stresses of the past gather within you. Jesus shows you a large vase and tells you to leave the past's sting there. Almost as though pulling out a substance, you take the shame and hurt from your chest and stomach and toss them into the vase. Then Jesus picks up the vase, embraces it, and takes it into his heart, where it disappears in a living flame of love. Then you ask Jesus, "Clear my vision that I may see people and things as they are and not just through the lens of the past." Jesus kisses each of your closed eyelids, then you open your eyes and see with sparkling clarity.

14

God Can Wipe Away Our Tears Forever

When you pass through waters, I will be with you;
through rivers, you shall not be swept away.
When you walk through fire, you shall not
be burned, nor will flames consume you.
ISAIAH 43:2

So many things make human life so wonderful. Nevertheless, many things in human life make it seem futile. Pain, suffering, and death can confound you. Like most people, you likely make every effort to isolate yourself from their sting. The reality is that suffering is part of the human condition. To be human means to feel pain, to suffer, and ultimately to die.

People may tell you to trust God and not to be afraid! However, that admonition alone would not alleviate your stress, your fears, your pain. Suffering and death reside in every fiber of your being. Christ embraced your humanity and every aspect of it. He feared, suffered, and died. He knows how you feel because he has felt it. There is more to all of this than just pain, suffering, and death. There is the promise of life eternal.

When you suffer and feel deserted, Christ draws very near to you, so that amid your suffering, you now have a brother who can taste the dregs of your distress, and you are never truly alone. His love can burn within you even in the hardest of times. He stands ready to console you, weep with you, wipe away your tears.

When I was a little boy, four or five years old, and I skinned my knee or stepped on a tack, I would run to my parents. Mother would wipe away my tears with her tender feminine hands. My father would wipe away my tears with his rough electrician's hands. It is an amazing thing to grasp that the same hands that made the cosmos can, one day, wipe away our tears into eternity.

Never deny your suffering or soft-pedal it, walling it off deep inside you where it can turn toxic and affect your whole personality. Instead, gather up your troubles and spread them before God. Suffering plays a role in your growth. Suffering ripens you, and when you take it to God, it can carve a huge space in your heart for compassion. You feel more keenly the sufferings of others who undergo trials. Suffering can midwife the birth of truly selfless love.

Prayer

Dear Jesus, take me up into the arms of your merciful love.
In times of sorrow and suffering, may my prayer to you
be like the voice of a child in the night to her mother,
summoning her tender care. Amen.

Guided Meditation

A great inner hush of comfort can flow over you from Christ's heart to yours. Jesus stands in front of you and tells you, "I love you in the silence with a love too great to speak. Enter into the holy stillness with me holding your hand. Let me now still your heart." Slowly enter into the quiet. Notice your breath: let it soothe you and remind you of the breath of the Spirit...Jesus says to you: Each time you breathe out, you breathe out stress. Each time you breathe in, you breathe in the restfulness of my presence. Let the fountain of my love pour down over you. Grasp my hand; slowly feel the place in my hand where the nail was. Let my love flow from my hand all through your arm, your shoulder, the whole of you, until body and soul are saturated in the warmth of my caring love. Rest awhile in the stillness with me.

15

God's Forgiveness Eases Our Stress

We are overcome by our sins;
only you can pardon them. PSALM 65:4

God is a lavish forgiver. That great evangelical preacher of the nineteenth century, Henry Ward Beecher, said, "God forgives like a parent who kisses the offense into everlasting forgetfulness."

God's forgiveness does for the human heart what sunshine does for a plant; it warms it and causes it to grow. Our hearts become tender and ready to forgive. Sadly, the idea of going to God to be forgiven holds little popularity today, even in many churches. It can be easy to blame others. You never become a failure until you blame someone else. Instead of blaming, rush into the wide-open arms of God, whose touch can pardon the wrongs of a lifetime. His forgiving embrace is the medicine that heals, the salve that calms, the touch that mends.

Take time each day to tell God about the shadows of your soul. If you are Catholic or Orthodox, you can complete and seal that forgiveness by taking part in the Sacrament of Reconciliation. God's forgiveness sucks the poison from our wounds. God's forgiveness is the only medication that can remove our emotional scars.

Prayer

Dear Lord, your forgiveness warms my heart, makes me pure, and opens me up to feel the unfathomable tender compassion of your care. Help me candidly acknowledge my sinfulness, ways that I have hurt you or others, and ways that I have broken your commands. Help me to pour out to you any bitterness that I may harbor in my soul. I call upon your compassionate heart to help me forgive others as lavishly as you have forgiven me. Give me the wisdom to reconcile with others when reconciliation is possible. Amen.

Guided Meditation

Seat yourself in a comfortable chair and take time to grow still. Perhaps repeat over and over again the Jesus Prayer: "Lord Jesus Christ, Son of God, have mercy on me, a sinner." The love of God fills the room. You feel someone grasp your shoulders from behind. It is Jesus. Peace, calm, and assurance flow from his hands into you. You feel safe, so very safe. Take time to remember the last time you experienced the release of forgiveness. Perhaps it was the relief and joy of experiencing the Sacrament of Reconciliation. Maybe it was a time when someone in your life whom you hurt reached far inside their hearts and forgave you. Experience again the peace of that moment. Now Jesus moves from behind your chair and sits in a chair facing you. He takes your two hands in his. You know he wants you to search your heart for ways that you have hurt yourself, God, or others; for times that you have broken God's commandments. Tell him about your sins and experience his tender compassion and forgiveness.

16

Forgiving Others Relieves Stress

"When you stand to pray, forgive anyone against whom you have a grievance, so that your heavenly Father may in turn forgive you your transgressions." MARK 11:25

Archbishop Desmond Tutu wrote a book with the compelling title *No Future without Forgiveness*. That same phrase can be applied to all of us. None of us has a future without forgiveness.

One definition of forgiveness is refusing to allow negativity into our hearts and relationships because of something someone has done to us. When we hold on to resentment, we are the ones who hurt. Max Lucado calls resentment the "cocaine of emotions."

Resentment rips us apart. It spoils our relationships. When we forgive, we don't deny the hurt or minimize what has been done to us. Instead, with God's help and the help of others, we grieve, let go, and move on. Forgiveness usually does not happen immediately. It is a process. It takes time. Just wanting to start down the journey toward forgiveness is enough in God's eyes; he will lead us the rest of the way.

Learn to bless the one you might now resent. Begin to pray for that person. Begin to see that person as a struggling child of God, just as you are. Feel with them. Walk in their shoes. What is their day like? What was their past like? Seeing the shared humanity of one who has hurt us can help us on the path to forgiveness and peace.

Thomas à Kempis wrote in *The Imitation of Christ*: "To know all is to pardon all."

Prayer

Dear Lord, you have forgiven me beyond measure. I call upon your compassionate heart to help me forgive others as lavishly as you have forgiven me. Give me the wisdom to find a way to reconcile with others when reconciliation is possible. Amen.

Guided Meditation

You are seated. Jesus stands beside you, holding your shoulder. Standing in front of you, you see someone you love who has wronged you. With Jesus' presence removing the hurt within you, pray for them. If you think you are ready to begin, look into the person's eyes and survey their face. What pain and difficulty in life do you think shaped them? Try to see the world from that person's perspective. You hear the person ask you, "What could I have done to love you better?" Answer their question. Then, only if you feel ready, tell them you are ready to begin the process of forgiving them. Only if you feel safe doing so, walk up to the person and clasp that person's hands in affection. Jesus comes and joins the two of you, placing a hand on your shoulder while placing a hand on the other person's shoulder.

17

His Presence
Can Meet You Amid
Your Troubles

"But I say to you, love your enemies,
and pray for those who persecute you."
MATTHEW 5:44

Sometimes it feels as if we are kicked when we are already down. It is painful to hear what people say about us behind our backs. It can be even worse when they say it directly to us. Donna was a server from my favorite restaurant who attended my church. I also considered her a friend. Though bright enough, she was born with dyslexia and had difficulties reading and writing. Overall, she was an excellent server with a caring personality that endeared her to many of her customers. She usually asked customers to repeat their orders to burn them into her memory. Most customers did so cheerfully, but one or two a week made fun of her. I knew it had to hurt.

One day, when I was eating at the restaurant, someone made fun of her in the booth in front of me. I considered intervening, but then thought a possible scene would make it worse. Instead, when the customer left, I motioned her over to me and told her she was the best server I had ever had. She told me not to worry because God helped her manage those situations. "He encircles me with his love and reminds me how many people love and appreciate me."

When others put you down about things you cannot help, as they did with Donna, think of times others have loved and affirmed you. Relive times when loved ones or friends spoke well of you—times you achieved despite difficulty. Take time, too, to let God embrace you. Think of times when his presence has met you with comfort amid your troubles.

Prayer

Dear Lord, I know that in your life here on earth others spoke ill of you, rejected you, mocked you. You turned to your Father, who affirmed you with infinite affirmation. You remembered the times you loved and healed people and, though imperfect, the love and support of your friends. There are times in my life when I am met with murmurs of rejection. Help me to sink my roots in your encouraging love. Help me to relive the times others have valued me.

Guided Meditation

You find yourself in a large field. The sun shines through an unclouded sky, brightening the green of the grass. People who have loved and appreciated you gather around you, telling you what you have meant to them. As you look out in front of you, you see some of the people who have disparaged you. You have a sense it is time to pray for them. Any unease you may feel disappears when Jesus steps behind you and puts his hands on your shoulders. You and the people who appreciate you join hands. You feel the power of all the caring that surrounds you fill you, and you pray for the people who have misunderstood or rejected you.

18

Move from Pain to Joy

*"So you also are now in anguish.
But I will see you again, and your hearts
will rejoice, and no one will take your joy
away from you."* JOHN 16:22

When we feel worried or stressed, it may seem there is no way out, that we are just stuck with our troubles. I felt that way for a while several years ago. I had let myself get over-booked. Nearly every week I had to travel across the continent for speaking engagements. I was so weary that my bones weighed me down like lead. I wondered if my talks were even helping people. In short, I was burned out.

A bright spot during that time was my frequent phone conversations with my Aunt Genella. A mother figure in my life, she was a woman of profound faith and thorough knowledge of Scripture. When she talked with me, her raspy voice filled with joy, she spoke of all the things that made her happy that day. On the face of it, it would seem as though she had little to be happy about. Paralyzed from a devastating stroke and in a nursing home far from three of her four children, she had to depend on others for the basics of life. Yet little things like the sun coming in through a window brought her delight.

I told her about my stress. She listened sympathetically and then she said, "Eddie, you have so much to be pleased about." It dawned on me that she had so much more wrong in life than I did, yet she delighted in the signs of God and beauty all around her.

I grasped how much I had been dwelling on the hard parts of my life. Realizing how much I was concentrating on what I lacked and what I feared, I started to notice the many ways that God and the beauty of his creation surrounded me. My mood lifted.

We have a choice. So much of how we feel depends on our focus. We can focus on the negative or on all the ways God comes to each of us every day and be joyful. Which will you choose today?

Prayer

Dear Lord, you came that we might have life and have it abundantly. You know what it is like to have trouble, but even amid those troubles the delight of the Father, the delight of creation, and the delight you found in your friends lifted you. Lord, I have troubles, too. Sometimes they seemingly grab me out of nowhere and throw me off center. When that happens, pour into me your marvelous joy. Fix my eyes on the beauty of each day you give me. Amen.

Guided Meditation

Sit quietly. Let the tender love of God gather around you. Relax in his presence. You see Jesus, holding a pitcher, walk toward you. He stands in front of you with a caring look on his face that calms you to the core. You feel so safe that you pour out your troubles to him. You feel emptied of their snares. Jesus puts his hand into the jar of living water of joy and sprinkles you with that water. Joy washes over you.

19

Bring Your Hopelessness to God

"He will wipe every tear from their eyes, and there shall be no more death or mourning, wailing or pain, [for] the old order has passed away."

REVELATION 21:4

Things like serious illness and death, the loss of a relationship, lost jobs, and missed opportunities happen to all of us. I remember when my young friend Jacob, a trainer at my local gym, came to the end of his hope. His parents, both doctors and agnostics, had expected much from him from the moment of his birth. They hoped he would follow in their footsteps and become a doctor. Good at physical things but not as intellectually endowed as his parents, he finished high school with a D average, not high enough for college. His parents often told him outright that he was a failure. Then came the news that he had incurable Hodgkin's disease.

Jacob had never been exposed to the Church; like his parents, he was an agnostic. In despair, having nowhere else to turn, he thought he would try God. At first his prayer was simply, through tears, "God, if you are there, help me." To his surprise, just uttering those words brought him great peace.

He broadened his prayers, pouring out his disappointments. An everlasting hope infused him. He read the Gospel of John, talked to a pastor at a local church, and was baptized. He reconciled with his parents and found many supportive friends in his parish who loved him for who he was, not what he had achieved.

The anguish of this world will not last forever. When despair overcomes you, remember that the time is coming when Christ will wondrously make a new heaven and a new earth. This is more than a belief; it is an experienced reality that can erupt inside you through the Spirit when hope seems to have abandoned you. Take time today to bring any hopelessness you feel to him so hope can grab you and take you into to a marvelous reality.

Prayer

Dear Lord, when I come to the end of my rope, you are there. I don't have to talk myself into hope, for you are hope, and when we encounter you, we encounter hope. When despair comes near me, enable me to open my mouth and tell you my troubles, inviting you into the situation. You took away the sting of death and the sting of desolation forever. You make all things bright and new. Fill me with that newness.

Guided Meditation

You are seated in your chair. The easing peace of God surrounds you. You breathe in that peace. Calm flows through you as you deeply relax each muscle. Now you go back in time to the tomb of Jesus, where he is buried. You become aware of the loss and the despair you may be feeling. They weigh you down. Suddenly, the earth rumbles. The stone in front of the tomb rolls away. Jesus stands at the entrance of the tomb. From his heart, bright heavenly light pours out, flowing directly into your heart, dispersing any hopelessness. Jesus speaks these words to you: "Behold, I make all things new."

20

Silencing Our Harsh Inner Critic

So let us confidently approach the throne of grace
to receive mercy and to find grace for timely help."
HEBREWS 4:16

Andrew was a young man in his late twenties who talked with me after a retreat session I gave in his parish. He attended church frequently but told me he was not good enough, was the worst sinner, and, as he put it, was "simply no good at all." In our long conversation, he didn't talk about anything particularly sinful. I probed further, asking him about his family growing up. It poured out that his father had severely abused him physically till he bled. And, even worse, his father verbally abused him, telling him he was a shame, worthless, simply no good.

Long after he left his father's house, he kept telling himself those judgmental words. It was as though if he could say worse things to himself than others could, their words would not hurt as much. After our conversation, Andrew started seeing a Christian therapist, developed a prayer life, and began bathing in the love of God. He was on the road to developing Godly self-esteem and mature faith.

Shame is when we have a harsh inner voice that tells us we are unworthy and unloved and that we should retreat and protect ourselves. In short, we might feel flawed and defective to the core. Have you ever felt unlovable, unworthy, or just not good enough? Most of us never had the same level of abuse or shame as Andrew. But so many of us have had enough that we struggle with shame. Whether we call it the inner critic or the superego, many of us have a judge within who nags us and is constantly on our case.

The answer to shame is wallowing in the free grace of God's transfiguring love. Pray, read Scripture, face your past, and you will be speeded on a pathway to self-esteem and a shame-free existence. The gospel frees us to be vulnerable and therefore to be liberated from our harsh inner judge because we are affirmed and cherished by the one who assumed our shame that we might enter into his joy.

Prayer

Dear Lord, your presence not only makes me holy; it also makes me beautiful. Enable me to see myself as you see me, not as my shame sees me. My shame was nailed to your cross; help me to leave it there. Help me let go of feelings of unworthiness, emotions that weigh heavily on my spirit, leading me to cower and act like I am damaged goods. You are eternal, and the cure you bring to me lasts forever. Amen.

Guided Meditation

Imagine that you are standing in a beautiful meadow, the green pastures spoken of in the Twenty-third Psalm. Bright sunlight fills the scene—the sunbeams of God's love. You hear footsteps rustle in the grass. You see a barefoot Jesus walking toward you. Imagine him in any way that seems good to you. He greets you with a firm, yet tender embrace. He says, "You are beautiful." He tells you some of the ways he sees you as beautiful. "In me, you can mute out forever the judge within that tells you that you are no good at all." Say to Jesus, "Lord, forgive the real sins I have committed. Through your grace, take away all the terrible things others said about me in my formative years that still nag at me." Rest in Jesus' embrace a long while.

21

Resplendent Signs of His Mercy

Blessed be the God...who encourages us
in our every affliction, so that we may be able
to encourage those who are in any affliction
with the encouragement with which we ourselves
are encouraged by God. 2 CORINTHIANS 1:3–4

For us, as for an oyster, every wound can become the origin of a pearl. God's comfort transfigures hurts, turning them into resplendent signs of his mercy. And our personal experience of his comfort makes us tender toward the failures and sorrows of others.

We call it empathy when one person feels the pain of another. There is something far deeper and richer than empathy in that Great Heart which gathers into itself all hearts. It is a simple and profound truth that the Being that underlies all our beings in our afflictions is afflicted.

His fellow feeling takes the sting of sorrow and makes it possible for us to gather our tears into healing reservoirs that shall be to us the sources of many a blessing—not only for us but for others, too.

As William Blake so beautifully put it in "On Another's Sorrow":

> *Think not thou canst sigh a sigh,*
> *And thy Maker is not by;*
> *Think not thou canst weep a tear,*
> *And thy Maker is not near.*

God's compassion soothing our hearts makes it possible for us to let the pain of other humans affect us and to pour out the same compassion on them that God poured out on us. In short, when we let God love us in our depths, we can love others in the depths of their pain, too.

Prayer

Dear Lord, you took my afflictions upon you in the agony of your humiliation, torture, and death. You catch my tears. Sometimes it is hard for me to walk through a day without the hurt of stress bothering me. Remind me always that your love can embrace me, for you have felt what I feel. Your compassion for me reaches beyond the heavens. Open my heart to your embrace. Send your Spirit on me, that I may become a conduit to your compassion for others. Amen.

Guided Meditation

Allow the calm of God to sweep over you. You breathe in his love; you breathe out your afflictions. Jesus walks into your room. You stand to greet him. You gently become aware of some of the hurt that dogs you. You see his wounds. The light of heaven shines brilliantly from those wounds. Like Thomas, you touch the wounds, placing your hand in his wounded side. He embraces you, his wounded side on your side, his nail-torn hands touching your back. You know he has felt what you feel. You are profoundly understood. Your hurts slip away, and you vow to love other people with that same compassion.

22

God Can Do Mighty Things

"Amen, I say to you, if you have faith the size of a mustard seed, you will say to this mountain, 'Move from here to there,' and it will move. Nothing will be impossible for you."

MATTHEW 17:20

God does mighty things. He came in the burning bush. He led Israel out of captivity. He appeared to Isaiah in the Temple. In Jesus, God became fully human, working miracles, feeding the five thousand, walking on water, healing the blind and the lame. God continued to do mighty deeds throughout the centuries, working miracles through the apostles, raising up saints like Francis of Assisi and Mother Teresa who changed the world. He can perform mighty things in us, too, if we but let him. He can work wonders in us.

I have seen it happen in people scores of times. I think of a young single woman who used prescription opiates to numb her to the dysfunction within her family. She felt helpless. As far as she could see, there was no way out. God deeply touching her on a parish retreat gave her the courage to go into rehab and start recovery. She soaked herself daily in God through prayer. His closeness planted a warmth and kindness in her to the point that she exuded God. Anger and distress slipped away, and she was able to reconcile with her siblings and parents.

In the silences, we can hear God's still, small voice, a voice that changes us and dissolves our sorrows. And when we follow that voice, God can so fill our personalities that the world can change around us.

In our own time and way, through his Spirit, we can be God's instruments in working mighty deeds. In soaking in his presence, our sorrows diminish as the snow does with the coming of spring.

Prayer

Dear Lord, remind me that not only do you soothe my hurts, but you also send me out in mission. When I draw close to you, you give me the power to move mountains of misunderstanding to reconcile and spread your love to others. Mighty things like changed families, changed parishes, changed workplaces happen when I soak myself in you. Give me the courage to listen to your voice and follow it to do mighty deeds. Amen.

Guided Meditation

Allow the presence of God to ease, relax, and calm you. A shower of light, the visible "Shekinah" glory of God rains down on you, soaking you with the presence of God. You see yourself go out and become an instrument of change for the world around you. You love better, and you are inspired to do the works of mercy, going out to those the world turns its back on. You seek ways to feed the hungry, befriend the lonely, and embrace the rejected.

23

Letting God Break the Chains of the Past

I praise you, because I am wonderfully made;
wonderful are your works!
PSALM 139:14A

We live in a fractured world where emotional wounds are inescapable. We may never stop thinking about the past, but we can decide how we look at it.

We all bear wounds from the past. I call them soul wounds. Perhaps a close friend cut us off forever and we don't know why. Infidelity in a marriage. Neglect and harm from those who were supposed to love us when we were children. Not feeling loved by our parents. We may even have experienced violence or sexual abuse from someone close to us.

An easy mistake we can make is to think, as believers, that we should always be happy and peaceful, beautiful examples of what it means to be Christ's followers. But such perfection is rarely the case. We are fearfully and wonderfully made, but growing into that is a process.

Shame and pride can lead us to conceal our wounds from ourselves, others, and God, cover them with a sheet, and hope they go unnoticed. Accepting that we have wounds is the essential beginning point for healing.

Nothing on earth can truly heal our wounds but God. Only the Paschal Mystery, the life, death, and resurrection of our Lord, his immense compassion, can heal the wounds of our souls. Because of what God has done for us, we can proclaim to the world, "With his wounds we are healed."

God's wish for us is wholeness and abounding joy. His delight is to see us fully alive. That process starts with us handing over our hurts into Jesus' hands. And Jesus invites us to do just that, saying, "Come to me, all you who labor and are burdened, and I will give you rest" (Matthew 11:28).

We can also allow the Holy Spirit to reconstruct our wounded hearts. Jesus called the Holy Spirit the comforter. He is also the weaver who can knit us back together again. The Spirit can still our souls with God's tenderest mercies. All that is asked of us is to give him access to our souls.

Prayer

Dear Lord, your love for me is far vaster than I can conceive, strong yet tender, approachable, and near. Touch my wounded parts with your soothing hand. Give me the strength to unlatch the doors of my heart so you may enter. Be with me daily in this journey of healing.

Guided Meditation

Jesus enters the room. He stands behind you and places his hands on your shoulders. You grow quiet, still, relaxed, and at ease. His touch is firm and reassuring. A light surrounds him, and you feel it surround you, too. This light makes you calm and warm. You sense an eternal love entering your life through Jesus' hands. It fills your body as well as your soul. You sense your hurts passing into Jesus' hands. What are some of those hurts? Jesus speaks to you: "It's human to have hurts. Acknowledge and name them, tell them to me, and know that as you name them, you turn them over to my infinite care."

24

Give Your Pain to Jesus

Have no anxiety at all, but in everything,
by prayer and petition, with thanksgiving,
make your requests known to God. Then the
peace of God that surpasses all understanding
will guard your hearts and minds in Christ Jesus.
PHILIPPIANS 4:6–7

Have you ever been assaulted by stress in the midst of your daily life? It may be tension from an overloaded schedule or anxiety from old hurts nagging you as you go about your day. It could be worry for your children or friction over relationships. You may not even be sure what it is; you just know you are pained. It is at such times that Jesus stands ready to understand and to soothe.

For example, imagine that you are the parent of a seven-year-old daughter who has just returned home from school. She rushes in to where you are seated, tears pouring down her cheeks, anguish written in her face. You wonder if she bruised herself in an accident or if something upsetting happened at school. Your daughter is too upset to tell you what is wrong right away. You open your arms and guide her into

HOLDING GOD'S HAND

your embrace. She says to you simply, "It hurts." You don't give her advice. Instead, you wisely say, "It hurts. I know it hurts." That is all she needs to hear right then. She relaxes in your arms, and peace overcomes the two of you. There is time later for details, but in that instant, you know you need to acknowledge that the hurt is real and comfort her.

So it is with Jesus. When we come to him with distress, maybe not even knowing the source of it, he will always respond by letting us know that he knows it hurts and swooping us into his comforting arms.

He knows our pain because he entered into all our hurts in his life on earth and in his passion. The comfort of his enveloping arms comes from the depths of eternity.

Prayer

Dear Lord, I am anxious at times: sometimes a little bit, at other times more. I can feel so alone when worry takes hold of me. At such times, help me to turn to you and simply say, "Lord, it hurts. You have experienced worry and distress, and you understand my hurt. Guide me throughout this day and teach me to run into your arms."

Guided Meditation

Imagine yourself seated in a chair. You see yourself surrounded by light: the pure light of the love of God, the light that showed on the mountain of transfiguration, the light of the new Jerusalem descending from heaven. The light relaxes you, brings you peace. Tension flows out of you into the light. Tight muscles relax in the light. Your arms, your legs, your whole body grow limp with the relaxation the light brings. You feel you are loved by the immensity of eternity. Talk to God. Let him know what hurts and then rest back in his arms.

25

Take Heart in Times of Trouble

Consider it all joy, my brothers [and sisters],
when you encounter various trials, for you know that
the testing of your faith produces perseverance.
And let perseverance be perfect, so that you may be
perfect and complete, lacking in nothing.

JAMES 1:2–4

Jesus says that "in the world you will have trouble, but take courage, I have conquered the world" (John 16:33). People get sick and die. People lose jobs and relationships fail. People end up living on the streets. We all have real trouble that cannot be pretended away.

Jesus knew this because he knew trouble, more trouble than we will ever know: rejection, mockery, betrayal, unjust suffering, and death. That's why he can help us.

Jesus also tells us to take heart because he has overcome the world. He loves us without measure. He loves tenderly. He has promised to walk beside us in the trouble, to carry our luggage of woe, to weep with us when we need to weep. If we cling to him, we can feel his love more intensely in the height of our tribulations. This is what he meant by taking heart.

St. James says that such testing "produces perseverance...so that you may be perfect and complete, lacking in nothing" (James 1:4). Troubles endured hand in hand with Jesus give us depth and great compassion for others. Helen Keller said, "We could never learn to be brave and patient if there were only joy in the world."

Due to a birth injury, I was have a cognitive visual spatial disability. Before it was properly treated, there were times I carried this weight on my own and was failing at life. I clung to Christ because there was no other place to cling. So often when troubles again came my way, I found deep rest on his bosom and a love that encircled me, infusing me with the heights of hope. He can do that for all of us when we run to him in our troubles.

Prayer

Dear Lord, guide me in taking my troubles to you. It is so hard at times, but I know you encountered countless people in trouble. You loved Zacchaeus and broke his deep isolation. You sent the woman with the hemorrhage on her way healed, loved, and happy. You healed the man born blind, giving him the precious gift of sight. I know you can likewise meet me in my troubles. I know you will ever walk by my side.

Guided Meditation

You are one of the multitude coming to Jesus. You see the lame now walking, the lonely embraced by him, the despised welcomed by him. Your turn comes to meet with Jesus. He reaches out and takes both your hands in his hands. You feel his healing compassion spread from his hands to yours, filling your body. Your anxieties just slip away. Tranquility rules your heart. He invites you to tell him about one of your troubles. You share your burden with him, and the lightness of joy-filled hope permeates you.

26

When Troubles Pile Up, God Is There

"Do not let your hearts be troubled.
You have faith in God; have faith also in me.
In my Father's house there are many dwelling places...
And if I go and prepare a place for you,
I will come back again and will take you to myself,
so that where I am you also may be." JOHN 14:1-3

My friend Julie, a woman in her early sixties, faced trouble all her life. Both of her parents had been abusive alcoholics and, as she put it, she was raised in foster homes "without much warmth." A loving cousin, not much older than she, took her in when Julie reached eighteen, providing much of the caring nurture she had missed growing up. She also took Julie back to church, where she fell in love with the Bible and the sacraments. God tenderly began to heal her broken places. Some years later, her cousin died of cancer. The gospel at her funeral Mass was from the first part of the fourteenth chapter of John, where Jesus tells us to not be troubled because we have eternal glory with him.

The truth behind those verses dosed Julie with comfort grounded in the everlasting. Her personality began to glow with God's love. This did not mean her troubles were over. Julie married; she had a son who died in his forties of a heart attack, soon followed by her husband's death in a car accident. However, that reality of tasting and experiencing the glory of God eased the sting of those troubles.

When we are in a dark room with no light, it is scary and confusing. It is so easy to trip over objects we can't see or to bump into things. Just switching on the light brings brightness and the ability to see clearly. Whenever we find troubles darkening our lives, we can remember that eternal life swallows up all sorrows. We can ask Jesus to give a taste of that light and life right here and now.

Prayer

Dear Lord, hard things can come in my life, such as trouble in my family, conflicts at work, loneliness, loss. So many things can pile up on me and darken my life. You have promised to light that darkness with your presence, not only right now but forever. Help me to grasp with every particle of my body and my whole soul your eternity, which touches me every time you touch me. Infuse me with a sense of forever that can soothe my soul, calm my mind, and fill me with unspeakable hope.

Guided Meditation

As you think about your difficulties, you vividly remember when Thomas, full of the darkness of doubt, confusion, and fear, put his hand into Jesus' resurrected side. The eternal brilliance of that moment lighted his life and sent him out as a mighty apostle. *You, too, put your hand into Jesus' resurrected side when you receive the Eucharist.* Know what it is you are doing. Each time you pray, eternity can descend within you. Now, in your imagination, place your hand in his side and let eternity brighten your soul.

27

God Can Ease Our Worries through People

*Each looking out not for his own interests,
but [also] everyone for those of others.
Have among yourselves the same attitude
that is also yours in Christ Jesus.*

PHILIPPIANS 2:4–5

Saint Augustine wrote, "The love with which we love God and love one another is the same love." Mature spirituality involves experiencing God in human relationships as well as in solitude. People can ease, comfort, and console us when our worries drag us down. Prayer and people belong together. Relationship is not a means to a goal; it *is* the goal.

We relate to one another not to win a war, not to implement a program or finish a project, but because it's our eternal calling. Amid the earthly coarseness of daily life, amid our shared humanity, people can become channels of God, lifting our burdens.

Think about the people who have touched you with God's touch. Perhaps they don't consciously know this. Perhaps they are not even outwardly religious people, but they have been a sign of God's love and a means of his love. They incarnate God's caring, enflesh it, and make it tangible. Many little saviors have incarnated the love of the one Savior.

The apostle Paul, in beginning and closing his letters, often said, "I think of you whenever I pray to God" (see Philippians 1:3).

Like Paul, we can remember people in our prayer and the times they helped us experience closeness and strength. Remembering brings those healing times into the present. In our prayer, we can experience again the people who have been to us the means of God's love.

Remembering brings those healing times into the present. In our prayer, we can experience again the people who have been to us channels of God's love. We can practice loving people in our prayer. We can bring hurt relationships to a loving God for mending.

Prayer

Dear Lord, you came so close to us in Jesus. Through him you showed us how to relate to you and to others. As I strive to love others, show me that I am not alone. Your hand in mine, you accompany me on our journey of loving and relating to others if I but ask you to join me. You pour your unfathomable love upon me. Help me to be a conduit of this love to others. You are the sunlight that heals as it warms. Help me to be a mirror that reflects this light to others.

Guided Meditation

In your imagination, picture Jesus standing beside you. You take his hand. You feel the place where the nail was, and you are reminded that that is how much he loves you. Healing warmth from his hand passes up from your hand into your arm, into your entire body, until you are flooded by warm, healing love. Carry your thoughts back to times when other people have consoled you, have comforted you, have looked to your interests, have really emptied themselves in a self-less way for you to experience the tenderness of God's love. Remember the sights, the sounds, and the feelings. God loves you like that, but infinitely more. Whenever fear or worry constrict your chest in anxiety, remember when another's touch has calmed you. Thank God for them and let their love remind you of God's love.

28

Seek Perfect Peace

With firm purpose you maintain peace;
in peace, because of our trust in you.
ISAIAH 26:3

For many of us, our greatest opponent is our fear. Fear limits our tomorrows and troubles our todays. It can take the zest of life out of us, often leaving us filled with dread. When fear dominates us, worry and stress pile up.

When I think of fear, my mind turns to the Gospel of Luke, chapter eight, where Jesus calms the storm. Rembrandt painted a picture of this scene, *The Storm on the Sea of Galilee*. A close look at the painting shows fourteen people huddled in the boat: twelve disciples plus Jesus. That makes thirteen. Who was the fourteenth? Rembrandt! He had painted himself into the picture.

Each time we read or hear this story of Jesus calming the storm, each of us can put ourselves forward as the fourteenth person. All of us must face our own storm, and Jesus can bring peace and calm as he did to the disciples.

In the midst of this scene, Jesus asked the disciples why they were so afraid. "Where is your faith?" (Luke 8:25).

Faith means saying yes to God's boundless love and constant peace. In short, it means turning our attention to him.

As Isaiah says, "With firm purpose you maintain peace; in peace, because of our trust in you" (Isaiah 26:3).

Prayer

Dear Lord, you alone can bestow the peace that passes all understanding. You can calm all the raging storms, inside and out, with the stillness of your perfect peace. In their panic, the disciples cried out, and you calmed the thunder and waves. May I, like the disciples, cry out to you when I am terrified and have forgotten for a while that you are in the ship with me. Help me to keep my mind focused on you, the one who has overcome all tempests. Remind me to touch you, to talk to you, and to center my soul on you the way a frightened child encircles a caring parent. Help me to spread this peace to all of those around me. Teach me to calm the wave of those most in need of peace, like you do.

Guided Meditation

Relax in God's presence. Let your muscles untighten and your mind grow calm. Search within your heart and see if any storms are raging. See Jesus in his long robe standing in front of you. Look on that face that shines with perfect peace. See his concern and compassion for you in his open arms. Let your gaze rest on him. Name the biggest storm in your life. Tell him about the dread. Ask him to calm the storm. He lifts his arm and says, "Peace. Be still." Touch his garment and feel that all is calm.

29

Give God Your Loneliness

"I will never forsake you or abandon you."
HEBREWS 13:5

We live in a culture of social media and cell phones. It is ironic to be connected to so many yet lack genuine companionship. We live in one of the loneliest times in the history of humanity. We were created for relationships, yet it seems easy for loneliness to creep into our lives like a lingering illness.

Do you feel lonely? Do your relationships lack quality and depth? Mother Teresa once said, "Loneliness and the feeling of being unwanted is the most terrible poverty."

Jesus spent many long hours in the anguish of loneliness in Gethsemane. He specializes in loneliness and knows how to help you in your loneliness. He experienced the absence of the Father so you would never be separated from his presence. He promised those who follow him, "I will never forsake you or abandon you" (Hebrews 13:5).

No matter how deep the pit of loneliness, God can provide a ladder out. One thing loneliness can do is drive us into the companionship of God. We can never be truly alone because he is with us. The God of the Universe needs and wants our friendship.

When we draw close to God, we enter into an eternal relationship that takes away all loneliness. As we develop this friendship with God, I believe we will find it easier to find human companionship. Involvement with the Church also breaks loneliness. Yes, the Church is messy and human, but over the decades I have found it a wonderful messiness.

Prayer

Dear Lord, I have had times of loneliness. Sometimes it seems that the people around me no longer care. Remind me that you care and that you entered the anguish of loneliness for all our sakes. Lead me daily to invite you in as my companion and friend. You, Lord, fill my needs. May you guide me in the pathways of deepening my relationships and making new relationships when needed. Amen.

Guided Meditation

Allow the Holy Spirit to bring the deep relaxation of an eternal love. Your body and soul relax as you wait in the stillness for a while. You stand and imagine Jesus standing in front of you. He says to you, "I want to know the hurt of any loneliness you may feel. Tell me about it." You tell him about it. He embraces you, with tears in his eyes, and says, "Pour out to me daily any anguish from loneliness you feel. My love will heal your anguish of isolation."

30

The Gift of Tears Cleanses Our Souls

*Those who go forth weeping, carrying
sacks of seed, Will return with cries of joy,
carrying their bundled sheaves.* PSALM 126:6

I met James during a mission trip. He did not regularly attend church, but a cousin brought him to a retreat Deacon Robert and I were leading. His business was a success, but he did not feel any happiness in that success. It was hard for him to feel any emotion. He had stopped attending church because he no longer felt God's presence as he had done in childhood. God seemed far away.

At the end of the morning session, Deacon Robert led a meditation with sacred music in the background, encouraging people to grow still. Then he asked the people to imagine Jesus seated next to them with his arm around them, spreading his love through their arms and filling their hearts. As James meditated, I saw tears streaming down his face. I talked with him afterward. He said, "When I imagined Jesus, I told him my heart is like a desert. I said, 'I need you to touch me. I need your love so much.' At that moment, tears began flowing uncontrollably, like a dam had burst, and I felt again, felt

God." His tears reminded me of the waters that break just before a woman gives birth. His life was changed.

As Frederick Brotherton Meyer, a Baptist pastor and evangelist, phrased it, "Tears are the material out of which heaven weaves its brightest rainbows. Tears are transmuted into the jewels of better life." Some experts say tears are a way the body lets go of chemicals built up by stress. I would add that tears cleanse us when we are profoundly touched. The Church has prayers for the gift of tears. May we be open to that gift.

Prayer

Lord, soften my heart. Fill me inwardly with tenderness in your great mercy. And if it is time for me, help me to express that tenderness in tears. Give me the gift of weeping away my anxiety when it is right to do so. Help me weep with compassion with those in need, a compassion that sets me to helping and soothing others' hurt. Amen.

Guided Meditation

Let your heart grow still. Let the peace of an everlasting love take hold in your soul as your limbs loosen up, your torso relaxes, and your soul is flooded by God's calm. Imagine that you are in a different place, a different time: the Holy Land during the time of Christ. See the woman who tenderly washes Jesus' feet with her tears. Pray for a gift of devotion and adoration equal to that woman's.

31

God's Compassion Frees Us from Past Trauma

"For I will restore your health;
I will heal your injuries."
JEREMIAH 30:17

Some of us have acute deep-seated pain, even agony, over terrifying events we went through or witnessed. Some call this post-traumatic stress disorder. Traumatic stress is a fact of life. Soldiers return from combat and their families deal with the painful aftermath of war. One in five Americans has been molested. One in four grew up with parents who were dependent on harmful drugs or alcohol. As many as one in four couples have engaged in physical violence.

Symptoms can include gut-wrenching anxiety, flashbacks, near uncontrollable rage or terror, and horrifying nightmares. Many let the trauma define them, resulting in major stress, worry, and fear. They may become addicted to alcohol and drugs. Most carry deep shame in their hearts.

The Scriptures show us a God who can change us, lead us

out of the deep valley, and create a beautiful life for us. He can break the chains that bind us to the trauma.

As an abuse survivor myself, I can say that nothing will mend our fractured hearts more than wallowing in the love of God. Dosing ourselves on comforting Scripture is part of our pathway. Taking a sunbath in God's compassion is the key that unlocks our recovery and allows us to move on. In addition, developing a network of supportive people in your life is essential. Please also consider seeing a therapist who can guide you through the process.

The more you are immersed in the ocean of God's love and include others who care in your journey, you will be speeded on a pathway to self-esteem and a shame-free existence. The gospel frees us to be vulnerable and therefore to be liberated from trauma. The one who embraces our shame and terror guides us ultimately into his joy.

Prayer

Dear Jesus, help me to know your presence by its soothing effects on our soul. Open your hand, Lord Jesus, and say to me, "I am with you; peace be unto you." Your presence absorbs my terror, my anguish, my deep-down hurts and dread. Remind me to tell you fully of the trauma of my past. Amen.

Guided Meditation

Let the deep relaxation that God brings sweep over you and pass through you. Softly relax your shoulders, your arms, your chest. Move deeper and deeper into profound calm. You are standing. Jesus walks into the room with you and stands facing you. His tranquility envelops you. Jesus looks at you, locking eyes with you. He places his palms upward; you can see the wounds where the nails were. Light now shines where the wounds of his hand are. He says softly but firmly, "Place your palms on mine." You do so. Your palms sense his wounds. Light is now streaming from them. Jesus says to you, "With these wounds, I took on the trauma and terror of your past, and resurrection light comes through them. The light of resurrection can flow from your wounds, too, transforming others, if you keep them soaked in my compassion."

32

God of All Comfort

Blessed be the God and Father of our Lord
Jesus Christ, the Father of compassion and
God of all encouragement, who encourages us
in our every affliction. 2 CORINTHIANS 1:3–4

The day my mother became ill, I was across the continent on a mission trip in Arizona. A phone call reached me with the news that my mother had become unresponsive and would likely die within a few hours. The next available flight was not until that night. She died while I was in flight. The next day, I went to visit her body with my dear cousins Jane and Betty. Tons of fear weighed down on my insides as I pondered what my life would be like without her. I would never see her again in this life.

My relationship with my mother had experienced beautiful healing in the last few years before her death, and she loved me more than words can measure or tell. Jane and Betty held me tight in their arms as I sobbed, joining their tears with mine. God was in their embrace, comforting me, too. The warmth of a caring and eternal consolation filled me. God's comfort alone can soothe and ease all fear.

Notice that Paul, in 2 Corinthians 1:3–4, calls God the God of all encouragement, or comfort, as other Bible translations put it. We need not limit God in his ability to comfort us. Let us allow God to comfort us in all our distresses where comfort is needed. There is no loss so dire that God cannot comfort. If we limit God's comforting hand, we won't allow God to reach the rock-bottom depths where consolation is so desperately needed. The Psalmist, moved by the intimacy of his God, put it this way: "Even though I walk through the valley of the shadow of death, I will fear no evil, for you are with me; your rod and your staff comfort me" (Psalm 23:4).

Prayer

*Dear Lord, when stress, worry, and fear lead me
into the darkest depths, you can warm me, encourage me,
and bring hope. In those times, you let me lean on your
everlasting arms. In Jesus, you have touched the depths of
suffering. Surround me with your larger-than-everything
love. As a mother consoles her child, O Gracious One,
console me. May your Spirit always remind me to turn
to you when I walk through life's dark valleys.*

Guided Meditation

You are seated in your chair. Let the Spirit deeply soothe your body. Your body feels lighter and at ease. The comfort of God descends upon you, bringing great peacefulness. As you sit there, you remember scenes in which others have comforted you. Perhaps someone brought you a bowl of chicken soup when you were ill, or someone listened with care when you did not receive a promotion you were sure of. Maybe someone offered you understanding and friendship when you feared your teenager was going down dangerous pathways. Perhaps a relative gave you a warm embrace and looked on you with caring eyes as they listened to your worries. Think of a time you were alone and very afraid and you felt God's direct comfort in your heart, or times when God infused you with hope when no hope seemed possible to you. You hear God whisper in your heart, "The comfort of my love is vaster than you could ever imagine."

33

What Christ's Compassion Is Like

You, LORD, are a compassionate and gracious God, slow to anger, abounding in mercy and truth. PSALM 86:15

Think of a time when you were stressed or feeling alone and shared your feelings with a friend or family member who deeply understood you, leading you to feel at peace. What was it like to be listened to and understood? Perhaps you felt warm and loved. Maybe you felt your anxiety lift out of you and disappear into the clouds like a balloon rising upward. In that moment, you experienced compassion.

Perhaps you have had times when a friend, child, or spouse opened up to you and you handled them lovingly and well. Maybe you clasped a hand or took them in your arms, shared their tears, reflected their feelings back to them, or pointed them toward Christ's compassion. What was that like for you? Did your heart widen?

What you experienced when another met you with compassion or when you showed compassion to another is just a fraction of what Christ's compassion for you is like. Go to him boldly. Go to him now. When your feelings are tangled, Jesus' compassion can sort them out.

Prayer

Dear Lord, your empathy is far beyond my ability to conceive. You are more intimate to me than I am to myself, nearer to me than my heartbeat, more vital to me than my very breath. At times, my feelings get tied up in knots, and calm seems far away. At those times, let me taste your compassion, a compassion so divine yet so human that it imparts the peace that is beyond understanding.

Guided Meditation

Imagine that you are seated on the bank of a river, a vast river, an endless river, the river of God's compassion. You float in the river. The river holds your weight; you feel so light. Your muscles relax. Fear, tension, and anxiety leave your muscles as you are bathed in the endless love that is compassion. The undulations remind you of God's undulations of love within your body. The pain of a lifetime disappears in the living waters of the flowing river. The river passes by. You experience earlier scenes in your life when you felt compassion and peace. You float back to the riverbank and sit down again. Jesus comes and sits beside you. You share with him any emotions that came up during this prayer journey. After you have spoken to Jesus, he puts his arm around your shoulder, carrying you more deeply into his peace.

34

Give Your Fear
to God

*For those who are led by the Spirit of God
are children of God. For you did not receive
a spirit of slavery to fall back into fear,
but you received a spirit of adoption, through
which we cry, "Abba, Father!"* ROMANS 8:14-15

One of the sad consequences of the pandemic has been our constant tendency to deeply stress over the future. Maybe it is hard for you to ever feel safe. Perhaps you fear whom death may take away from you. Danger seems to lurk around every corner. Even when the pandemic eases, it is easy to be petrified of what world-altering event may be gathering on the horizon to break things apart again.

This fearsome stress can hurt and boil inside. Though you try hard to keep it from erupting, your throat may choke up a bit in ordinary conversation. You may stress so much that you have panic attacks.

Jesus tasted the anguish of profound stress as he approached his crucifixion. Yet, death did not grasp him forever. He died into his Father's arms and arose to the joyous strains of heaven and earth. In his suffering and rising, he took away the hurt of stress forever. In his resurrection, he offers you a sure medicine for all worry: his presence.

Take your bewilderment, your fright, and tell him about them. Pour them out, weep them out, shout them out. One way to do this is to read Romans 8 prayerfully and slowly before you talk to him about what bothers you. You have no stress rattling inside that he cannot convert into deep peace; no worry that he cannot remake into a profound tranquility. He loves you eternally.

Prayer

Lord, I cry out to you in my fear. Stress and worry are my constant companions. Shadows lurk around every corner. I fear what tomorrow may bring. Please shine your light into my darkness. Help me feel the relief and peace that only you can give me.

Guided Meditation

Jesus takes a chair and sits in front of you. You can tell by the look on his face that he cares about you very much. He is surrounded by subdued light, and this light surrounds you, too. Love and healing that cannot fully be expressed in words pass through the light, from Jesus to you. Your stress and worry just slip away. Pour out your feelings to him. There is no need to hold back, for he can absorb all the pain. Surrender to the peace that Jesus provides.

35

When You Feel Abandoned by God

"My God, my God, why have you forsaken me?"
MATTHEW 27:46

Jesus had been scourged, had a crown of thorns pierce his head, was forced to carry a cross through the streets, was stripped of his clothes, and then was hung on the cross. In the midst of this cruel torment, he cried out to his Father, "My God, my God, why have you forsaken me?" (Matthew 27:46). Jesus, in his humanity, knows what it is to feel abandoned by God. He knew the cross was a stepping-stone to the moment of ultimate glory, the resurrection.

There are times in our lives as well when we feel that God is nowhere to be found. We feel alone, desperate. Pain presses in on us on every side. There seems to be nowhere to turn. Our prayers go unanswered. Whom can we rely on when it seems that even God has abandoned us?

It is at those times that we are called to trust in God even when we cannot feel him. Our feelings are not always a true measure of reality. God is with us even when he seems to be absent. These times are a true test of our faith. The famous poem "Footprints in the Sand" illustrates this fact beautifully.

In that poem, a person looks over their life and sees two sets of footprints, their own and the Lord's, for much of their life, but in the times of deepest need, there is only one set of footprints. The person asks the Lord about this. Jesus replies, "It was then that I carried you."

God is always with us, especially at our times of greatest need, whether we can feel his presence or not. Jesus knew that God was with him in his darkest hour, even when he could not feel it. We, too, are called to trust in the midst of the darkness. Jesus is carrying us, supporting us, giving us strength in our hour of need, even when we cannot sense his presence. We, too, must believe that our time of pain and sorrow will come to an end, and we will experience the joy of resurrection.

Prayer

Dear Lord, when I feel alone and abandoned by God, help me to remember that you are always with me, that I can rest in the knowledge of your love and support even when I cannot feel it. Strengthen my faith that I may believe even when that faith is put to the test. Please carry me safely through the dark times of my life so that I may experience the light and joy of resurrection. Amen.

Guided Meditation

Quiet your soul and rest in the stillness. You see the Lord standing before you. He is surrounded by a holy light, which expands to envelop both of you. You breathe in the light. It fills you, warming you and comforting you. You feel safe and secure and loved in the Lord's presence. Jesus says to you, "I am always with you, every moment of your life. I will never leave you. Trust in my love for you. Know that I am near even when you do not feel my presence." Rest and take comfort in the presence of the Lord.

36

Let the Lord Wash Away Your Shame

*"Whoever believes in me...'Rivers of living water
will flow from within him.'"* JOHN 7:38

Have you ever felt ashamed? Maybe it was an indiscretion long ago, a disability, a job loss, or another reason. In Scripture, a deeply shamed woman washed the feet of Jesus with her tears (Luke 7:37–47). Even though others rejected her, Jesus welcomed her and treated her with tenderness. He had a way of drawing intimately near to him those who were full of shame.

One shame I almost never told anyone about for decades was that I flunked out of a Presbyterian theology school my third year. I was bright enough, but my disability, major neurocognitive impairment from a birth injury, caused me serious problems in completing my huge load of graduate work. In addition, I had big problems with daily activities like dressing and hygiene. Shame filled me every minute of every day.

One night, isolated and ashamed, I was racked with sobs over my situation. As the tears rolled, it was almost as though God spoke to me in the words of this Scripture: "Whoever believes in me...'Rivers of living water will flow from within him'" (John 7:38). My tears reminded me of the living waters God brings. I felt my shame slip away as the freshness of life-bearing water flowed within.

His presence abided with me during those hard times, and I prayed that my many tears might be a washing of his feet. God carried me through. I went on to earn a master's degree in theology and a doctorate, wrote nineteen books, and preached to hundreds of thousands of people.

The Lord can fill you with a fountain of living water as he lets you wash his feet with your tears. He can wash away your shame and make you whole.

Prayer

Dear Lord, you draw near to me even when I feel so far away, embarrassed, even ashamed. You offer to come home and stay at my house, just as you did with Zacchaeus, who was isolated in shame. Lord, you rush to me despite my shame. Give me the courage to allow your love to cleanse me white as snow.

Guided Meditation

You are seated in your chair. The presence of God fills the room. You feel the weight of your embarrassment and shame slip away into the Divine Presence. You see Jesus, barefoot, coming toward you carrying a towel. He asks you to slip off your shoes and socks. He begins to weep for you as your shame draws him intimately close to you. He washes your feet with his tears and dries them with the towel he is carrying. He kisses your feet. When he finishes, you are overcome with tears of intimacy and relief. You want to wash his feet. You take the towel and wash his feet with your tears. Instead of being a barrier, your shame has drawn him close.

37

Friendships Can Be Medicine for Our Stress

"Faithful friends are a sturdy shelter;
whoever finds one finds a treasure."
SIRACH 6:14

God created us so that we need people. One of the most important things we can do to handle worry, stress, and fear is to develop friends. Few things ease us like sharing our joys with a friend who listens well. A friend's hand on our shoulder relaxes and calms us in profound ways when we are hurting. Sharing the things of the heart with a friend who cares can be a breakthrough to eternity. Sure, people are flawed and difficult at times. But God can still come to us in them. We call these special heart friendships "spiritual friendships." They are a powerful elixir when our hearts are troubled.

Spiritual friendships—and all good friendships, for that matter—don't just happen; they take time and energy to build. Two acquaintances don't just decide to become spiritual friends. It is something that emerges from more ordinary, everyday friendship. Spiritual friendships come about when people are each on a journey to God and share their mutual journeys. In my own life, I have a special dear friend in Joanna Brunson. Though she lives a hundred miles away in Atlanta, we pray together by phone and share our connection with God. She has been a great medicine for my soul.

As Aelred, a medieval monk, puts it:

> No medicine is more valuable than a friend. He will be someone whose soul will be to us a refuge to creep into when the world is altogether too much for us, and someone to whom we can confide all our thoughts... He will weep with us when we are troubled and rejoice when we are happy. He will always be there to consult when we are in doubt. And we will be so deeply bound to him in our hearts that even when he is far away, we shall find him together with us in spirit. (https://www.azquotes.com/author/32527-Aelred_of_Rievaulx)

Prayer

Dear Lord, you have been a friend to each of us. In creation, you called the entire cosmos into friendship. In Jesus' friends, you gave us a model of friendship. By becoming one with us in the incarnation, you offered eternal friendship to each of us, your children. You have called us into friendship with one another. May I befriend others with the same love with which you befriended humankind. Lead me into spiritual friendships gently and gradually. Help me to commit to others just as you committed yourself to us. Help me to keep my love for others pure and life giving. Lord, help me to allow your love, the one love, to be the same love with which I love others and the same love with which I reach out to a hurting world.

Guided Meditation

Begin to slow down. Put on some soothing music and drift slowly into the depth of comfort that God offers everyone. Think of your current relationships with both friends and relatives. Watch scenes from those relationships. Is there joy there? Now see in your mind's eye what you can do to enhance those friendships. Now picture yourself where you are seated and a fountain flowing upward from your heart spilling out the love of God, the source of the fountain, on all your friends. Finally, picture the love you share with friends expanding and covering the whole world, especially touching the neediest, the sick, prisoners, and outcasts, causing the whole globe of the earth to glow with the love of God that powers your friendships.

38

Christ Offers Us Unending Peace

"Peace I leave with you; my peace I give to you.
Not as the world gives do I give it to you.
Do not let your hearts be troubled or afraid."

JOHN 14:27

Jesus came to bring us peace: deep-down, lasting peace. Even when the surface of the ocean rages in a tumult of waves and winds, far below the surface lies an unbroken calm. This is the kind of peace he offers.

When people try to comfort someone in sorrow, people usually use simple words. Moreover, when Jesus spoke to his disciples before he left them, he used the simplest words to calm their bewildered and worried hearts. He told them, "Peace I leave with you; my peace I give to you. Not as the world gives do I give it to you. Do not let your hearts be troubled or afraid" (John 14:27).

He offers us this same peace. Peace does not mean absence of conflict. When Jesus spoke these words of peace to his followers, everything was unsettled and chaotic around him. Some hated him and planned to kill him. Some spoke disgusting words to him, yet he knew a deep and enduring peace. He imparted this peace to his disciples, and, if you will let him, he can impart this peace to you.

Are things stormy in your life right now? Perhaps you have quarrels with those you love or with people at work, or your heart is disturbed because of disputes in the family. Jesus can anchor your soul in peace amid the disorder.

Many people toss and turn because of the tug-of-war in their hearts, but peace is not always easy to grasp. Learning to be content and quietly accepting whatever life tosses your way is another entrance into peace. St. Paul wrote: "I have learned, in whatever situation I find myself, to be self-sufficient. I know indeed how to live in humble circumstances; I know also how to live with abundance. In every circumstance and in all things I have learned the secret of being well fed and of going hungry, of living in abundance and of being in need. I have the strength for everything through him who empowers me" (Philippians 4:11–13).

The most important peace God can give you is the peace of his presence. You cannot be at peace in the very roots of your being unless you are at peace with him. On the surface, there may be times of delight, storms of energy, but unless you let God soak your inner being with his serenity, there won't be peace deep down.

Prayer

Dear Jesus, your heart breathes goodness and mercy over me. Walk with me in green pastures and lead me by the side of still waters. Soothe me, calm me, cradle me, saturate me in your peace so that I spread that peace, like a holy contagion, to everyone I meet. May your peace so envelop this world that clashing arms cease and the thunder of war is heard no more.

Guided Meditation

Take time and grow still. Let your breathing in and out remind you of the tranquility of Christ's peace. When you breathe in, breathe in his peace; when you breathe out, breathe out conflict. In the safety of Christ's presence, tell him about the storms in your life. Relive with him the conflict. Think of the peace he brought to the world and say a deep "yes" to his bringing you that same peace within you now.

How to Counsel with the Author Personally

I am a Board Certified Pastoral Counselor with a doctorate in clinical pastoral counseling. I can counsel people throughout the country by phone or Zoom.

My therapeutic style is warm, empathetic caring, friendly, and welcoming. Through listening, psychotherapy, and prayer, I will walk with you through any darkness, sadness, and confusion you may feel to the welcome of God's outstretched arms. Recovery after loss is a specialty of mine.

By facing your emotions, whatever they are, in counseling and prayer you can be guided into the utter tranquility of God's peace. Contact me for a free 20-minute appointment to discuss my counseling you.

Deacon Eddie Ensley, PhD, author

TO SET UP AN APPOINTMENT, EMAIL ME AT
pmissions@charter.net OR VISIT **www.eddieensley.com**

"I have known Eddie Ensley since he was a very young man, and he has always had passion and skill for healing real people with their real sufferings...you are being taught by a master who has practiced this healing work for most of his life."
RICHARD ROHR, OFM, author of *The Universal Christ*

I am grateful to Deacon Ensley for his continued ministry, and I pray that it will continue to bear great fruit."
BISHOP STEPHEN D. PARKES, my bishop (Savannah)